Quilt the Rainbow

A SPECTRUM OF 10 EYE-CATCHING COLORFUL QUILTS

Amber Johnson
of GIGI'S THIMBLE

Martingale®
Create with Confidence

Quilt the Rainbow:
A Spectrum of 10 Eye-Catching Colorful Quilts
© 2022 by Amber Johnson

Martingale®
18939 120th Ave NE, Suite 101
Bothell, WA 98011-9511 USA
ShopMartingale.com

Printed in Hong Kong
27 26 25 24 23 22   8 7 6 5 4 3 2 1

Library of Congress Cataloging-in-Publication Data is available upon request.

ISBN: 978-1-68356-195-8

MISSION STATEMENT

We empower makers who use fabric and yarn to make life more enjoyable.

CREDITS

PRESIDENT AND
CHIEF VISIONARY OFFICER
Jennifer Erbe Keltner

CONTENT DIRECTOR
Karen Costello Soltys

DESIGN MANAGER
Adrienne Smitke

TECHNICAL EDITOR
Ellen Pahl

PRODUCTION MANAGER
Regina Girard

COPY EDITOR
Melissa Bryan

BOOK DESIGNER
Angie Haupert Hoogensen

ILLUSTRATOR
Sandy Loi

PHOTOGRAPHER
Brent Kane

SPECIAL THANKS
Photography for this book was taken at:
Lori Clark's Farmhouse Cottage in Woodinville, Washington
The home of Tracie Fish in Kenmore, Washington
Happy Hollow Farm in Silvana, Washington

DEDICATION

To all of the artistic, talented fabric designers who create the beautiful fabrics that I simply can't resist, and to all of the inspiring fabric stores that make those fabrics easy to buy. Without you, this book would not exist!

To my grandmother Delma (aka Gigi), who taught me how to quilt more than 20 years ago. I miss you but think of you often as I carry on your love of quilting.

To my family and friends—thanks for always cheering me on!

Contents

Introduction

It's such a treat to visit an inspiring quilt shop and come home with beautiful fabric. I like to make scrap quilts, so I often purchase fat quarters in varying colors and prints when I'm buying just for fun. Fat quarters are just the right size to yield lots of different-size pieces and bring me the joy that only new fabric can offer—without too high of a price tag.

When I get home, I fold my new fat quarters just like the many other (partial or full) fat quarters I have on my shelves, and then I carefully place them on the existing stacks of fabric according to color. Sorting by color allows me to see what colors I have a lot of and what colors I lack. To be honest, after so many years of collecting fat quarters, I don't really lack any color!

I wrote this book for those of you who, like me, have colorful stacks of fabric just waiting to be enjoyed and stitched into quilts. *Quilt the Rainbow* provides 10 scrappy quilt designs to help you whittle down each color of your stash. Whether you buy fat quarters or yardage, you can use whatever cut of fabric you have on hand; the patterns in this book are scrap/stash friendly! Of course, each pattern could easily be made in a different colorway than what is shown (or in multiple colors). So have fun mixing and matching the patterns in this book with the colors of your choice as you quilt through your own rainbow of fabric!

Making Scrap Quilts

Working with dozens of scraps to create a beautiful quilt can be a bit messier and more time consuming than making a quilt from just a few fabrics. But, the results are worth it! In this section you'll find some techniques that help me be efficient and organized when it comes to scrap quilting. I've also included some hints about selecting fabrics for a scrap quilt.

Time-Saving Storage Tips

Here's my hit list of tips that help me keep my scraps under control and ready to use.

- Put a basket near your cutting table for tossing large pieces of fabric into until you're done cutting and have time to put them all away.

- Cut scraps for multiple projects at a time. For example, if I'm using fat quarters from my stash to make one scrap project with squares and another

with strips, I'll cut the pieces for both projects at once. Then I put the remainder of the fat quarters in the basket by my cutting table until I have cut everything I need for both projects. When I'm done, I fold all the fabrics from the basket and put them back into my stash.

- Cut multiple layers of fabric at a time. However, to ensure accuracy, I usually cut no more than two to four layers at once.

- Use a small rotating cutting mat and/or small rulers to make cutting small scraps faster and easier.

- When I have scraps measuring 8" square or less, I cut them into smaller squares and store them in clear boxes according to size and color. I start by cutting the largest size square I can get from each scrap and move down from there. I usually cut 5", 4", 3", 2½", 2", and 1½" squares. (The 1½" squares are destined for a postage stamp quilt that I have in progress as I write this book.) When I'm ready for a scrap project, I know exactly where to look. You could also cut strips to your desired width and/or length.

- I store scraps smaller than a fat eighth or fat quarter, but larger than 8" square, in large, clear glass storage jars. Look for jars that hold two gallons and are about 11" tall and 10" in diameter. They're cute and easily accessible. When you're ready to use fabrics from a jar, place the jar near your iron and ironing board so that you can give them a quick press as needed.

Limited green color palette   *"Anything goes" green color palette*

Choosing Fabrics

Each of the quilts in this book includes an assortment of fabrics that are in the same color family. It's OK to use lots of different shades of one color, or, if you prefer, you can try to keep your fabric selection to one shade of a particular color. There really is no right or wrong; it's up to your personal preference. Just know that if you want to use lots of different shades and tints of one color—the more, the merrier! A *shade* of a color is the pure color with black added. A *tint* is the pure color with white added.

Spread out your chosen fabrics and colors next to each other to make sure that you have a variety of everything, from color to print style. Repetition creates balance, so if there's one fabric that jumps out at you, either repeat it a couple more times with something similar, or remove it. The photos above show an example of fabrics in one particular shade of green and another example of a fabric selection in lots of shades of green.

Scrap quilts can use every color under the sun, or they can have a limited color scheme. I found that some of my scrap quilts started to look too similar because I was always using the same color scheme. To mix things up, I began trying out different color schemes with a limited color palette and found it very fun and satisfying. Sometimes it can be difficult to make a change from a favorite color

palette. If you'd like to challenge yourself, try pulling a crayon from a box or a paint chip from a bag without looking. Or find a photograph on Pinterest with colors that really speak to you.

To help you stretch outside of your box, examine your fabric stash to see what colors you have the most of and what colors you may want to add. If you don't have a lot of orange prints, it may be because you don't love orange. Or, maybe it's because a little orange goes a long way. Adding some new orange fat quarters or fat eighths to your existing stash is an easy way to build up your variety of prints in that color. Then challenge yourself to make a quilt incorporating some of those new orange fabrics.

Another great way to get a scrappy look is by swapping fabrics or blocks with friends, a local quilt guild, or an online group whose members all have a copy of *Quilt the Rainbow*. Select your favorite pattern, provide details about the color palette you're going for, and start sewing!

Pull three "surprise" paint chips from a bag to inspire a new color palette.

Swap fabrics, units, or blocks with friends to achieve an extra-scrappy look.

Any quilt in this book can become a rainbow quilt!

The quilts in this book will be cute in any colorway. I intentionally designed patterns that offer a lot of versatility to help you use up your stash. So feel free to make something similar to what is shown or make one of the patterns in a different color family. For example, if teal isn't your favorite color, you can certainly make the Seaside quilt (page 36) using the color scraps you have the most of, whether that's red or green or navy. You could even make some of the projects in just two fabrics if you don't love scrappy quilts. If you love colorful quilts, you could experiment with combining a variety of colors as I've done in the Star Studded rainbow quilt (page 62).

The possibilities are endless, and I can't wait to see what you come up with! Please tag me if you're on Instagram and like to post your projects. My username is @gigis_thimble, and I'd love for you to use the hashtags #gigisthimblepattern and #quilttherainbowbook.

Sew Delightful

Combined with white, red is a go-to color for many quilters and a winning classic. I've found myself burned out on red at times, but while making this big-block beauty, I fell in love with the color red all over again.

Materials

Yardage is based on 42"-wide fabric. Fat quarters measure 18" × 21". I found that nondirectional prints work best for this pattern, but of course it's up to you!

5½ yards of white print for blocks, sashing, and border

16 fat quarters of assorted red prints for blocks and sashing

⅞ yard of red diagonal stripe for binding*

8½ yards of fabric for backing

99" × 99" piece of batting

*If the stripe runs the lengthwise grain of the fabric and you want to cut binding strips on the bias, purchase 1⅛ yards.

Cutting

All measurements include ¼" seam allowances. Refer to the cutting guide, right, for the red prints; cut carefully to ensure that you get all of the required pieces from each fat quarter.

From the white print, cut:

2 strips, 20½" × 42"; crosscut into 24 strips, 2½" × 20½"

4 strips, 8½" × 42"; crosscut into 64 pieces, 2½" × 8½"

3 strips, 5½" × 42"; crosscut into 16 squares, 5½" × 5½"

12 strips, 4½" × 42"; crosscut into:

    64 squares, 4½" × 4½"

    64 pieces, 2½" × 4½"

13 strips, 2½" × 42"; crosscut 4 of the strips into

    64 squares, 2½" × 2½"

From *each* of the assorted red prints, cut:

1 square, 5½" × 5½" (16 total)

2 squares, 5¼" × 5¼"; cut in half diagonally to yield 4 triangles (64 total)

1 square, 4½" × 4½" (16 total)

4 strips, 2½" × 12½" (64 total)

13 squares, 2½" × 2½" (208 total; 7 are extra)

From the red diagonal stripe, cut:

10 strips, 2½" × 42"

Cutting guide

Making the Blocks

The instructions are for making one block. Repeat to make 16 blocks, using one red print in each block. Press seam allowances in the directions indicated by the arrows.

1 Draw a diagonal line from corner to corner on the wrong side of a white 5½" square. Or, use Diagonal Seam Tape (page 73) to avoid marking. Place

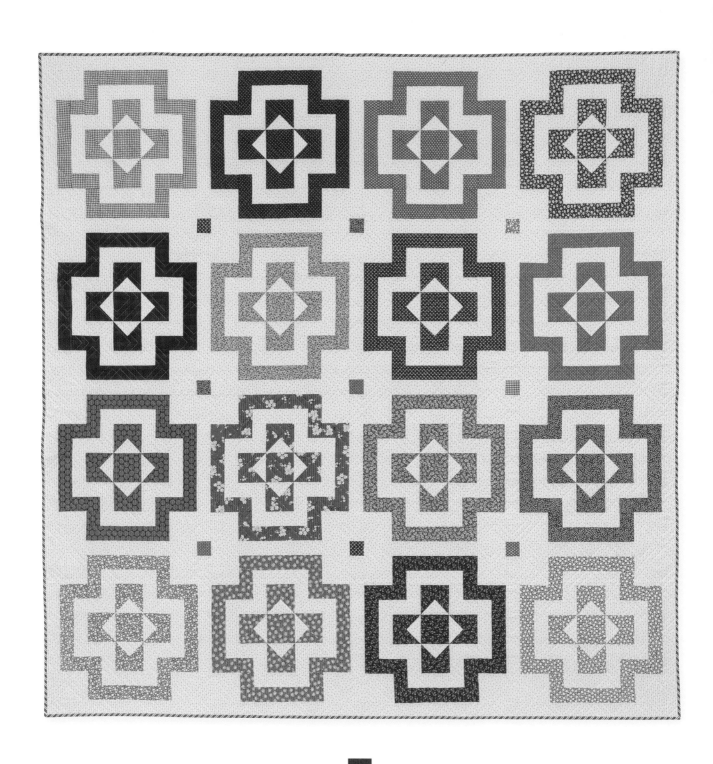

Pieced by Amber Johnson; machine quilted by Jen Ostler

FINISHED QUILT: 90½" × 90½" // **FINISHED BLOCK: 20" × 20"**

a marked square on top of a red 5½" square, right sides together. Pin the squares together and sew ¼" from both sides of the drawn line. Cut the squares into quarters diagonally to yield four pieced triangle units as shown.

Make 2 of each unit.

2 Sew together a unit from step 1 and a matching red 5¼" triangle along the long edges with right sides together. Make four units. Trim the units to 4½" square, including seam allowances, and set them aside.

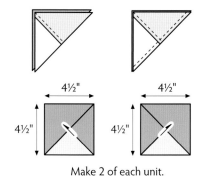

Make 2 of each unit.

3 Sew together a white and a red 2½" square. Make four units measuring 2½" × 4½", including seam allowances. Sew a white 2½" × 4½" piece to the bottom of each unit as shown, positioning the red square on the left in two of the units and the red square on the right in the other two units. The units should measure 4½" square, including seam allowances.

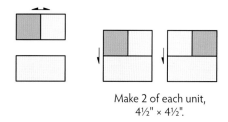

Make 2 of each unit, 4½" × 4½".

4 Sew a red 2½" square to each end of a white 2½" × 8½" piece. Make four units measuring 2½" × 12½", including seam allowances.

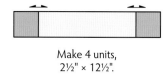

Make 4 units, 2½" × 12½".

5 Sew a red 2½" × 12½" strip to the top edge of each unit from step 4. Make four units measuring 4½" × 12½", including seam allowances.

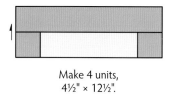

Make 4 units, 4½" × 12½".

6 Sew a white 4½" square to each end of two of the units from step 5. The units should measure 4½" × 20½", including seam allowances.

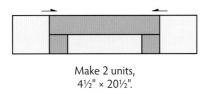

Make 2 units,
4½" × 20½".

7 Arrange one red 4½" square, the four units from step 2, and the four units from step 3 in three rows as shown. Sew the units and square together in rows. Sew the rows together. The block center unit should measure 12½" square, including seam allowances.

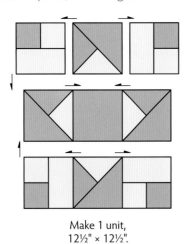

Make 1 unit,
12½" × 12½".

8 Sew the two units from step 5 to opposite sides of the center unit. Sew the units from step 6 to the top and bottom to complete an Economy Plus block. The block should measure 20½" square, including seam allowances. Repeat the steps to make a total of 16 blocks, one from each red print.

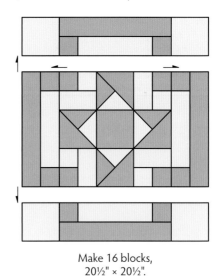

Make 16 blocks,
20½" × 20½".

Assembling the Quilt Top

1 Arrange four white 2½" × 20½" strips and three red 2½" squares as shown. Sew them together to make a sashing row that measures 2½" × 86½", including seam allowances. Make three rows.

Make 3 rows, 2½" × 86½".

2 Arrange four blocks and three white 2½" × 20½" strips as shown. Sew them together to make a block row that measures 20½" × 86½", including seam allowances. Make four rows.

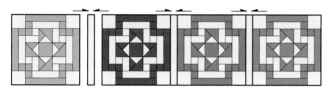

Make 4 rows, 20½" × 86½".

3 Referring to the quilt assembly diagram, sew the block rows and sashing rows together. The quilt center should measure 86½" square, including seam allowances.

Quilt assembly

4 Trim the selvages from the nine white 2½" × 42" strips. Sew the strips together end to end with a straight seam to make one long strip. Press the seam allowances in one direction. From the pieced strip, cut two strips, 2½" × 86½", and sew them to opposite sides of the quilt center. Cut two strips, 2½" × 90½", and sew them to the top and bottom. Press the seam allowances toward the border on all sides. The quilt top should measure 90½" square.

Another Option

If you'd like a smaller quilt, simply make fewer blocks. The quilt can easily be adapted to a 2 × 2, 3 × 3, 2 × 3, or 3 × 4 block layout for a wall hanging, baby quilt, or throw quilt.

Finishing the Quilt

Refer to "Finishing" on page 75 for details as needed.

1 Trim the selvages from the backing fabric and cut it into three pieces, approximately 42" × 102" each. With right sides together, join the pieces along the long edges to make a backing with vertical seams. Press the seam allowances to one side.

2 Layer the quilt top with batting and backing and quilt as desired. The quilt shown is machine quilted with the Diagonal Plaid pantograph by Patricia E. Ritter.

3 Use the red stripe 2½"-wide strips to make double-fold binding and then attach the binding to the quilt. Add a label, if desired.

Scrapology

For me, thinking of pink conjures sweet images like strawberries, hearts, and my favorite flower—peonies. This pattern, however, is so versatile that your quilt could transform from sweet to bold, depending on the color scheme you choose.

Materials

Yardage is based on 42"-wide fabric.

3 yards *total* of assorted pink prints for blocks and scrappy binding

3 yards of white print for blocks

3¼ yards of fabric for backing

57" × 77" piece of batting

Cutting

All measurements include ¼" seam allowances.

From the assorted pink prints, cut a *total* of:
144 squares, 3½" × 3½"
13 strips, 2½" × 20"
34 pieces, 2½" × 10½"

From the white print, cut:
3 strips, 10½" × 42"; crosscut into 48 pieces, 2½" × 10½"
11 strips, 5½" × 42"; crosscut into 72 squares, 5½" × 5½"
1 strip, 2½" × 42"; crosscut into 3 pieces, 2½" × 10½"

Making the X Blocks

Press seam allowances in the directions indicated by the arrows.

1 Draw a diagonal line from corner to corner on the wrong side of a pink square. Or, use Diagonal Seam Tape (page 73) to avoid marking. Place a marked square on one corner of a white square with right sides together. Pin the squares together and stitch on the drawn line. Trim ¼" from the stitching line. Repeat on the opposite corner with a different pink square. The unit should measure 5½" square, including seam allowances. Make 72 units.

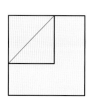
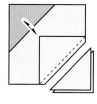

Make 72 units,
5½" × 5½".

2 Lay out four units as shown, striving for eight different pinks in each block. Sew the units together in rows and sew the rows together. The X block should measure 10½" square, including seam allowances. Make 18 X blocks.

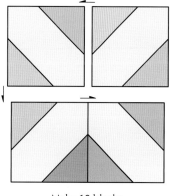

Make 18 blocks,
10½" × 10½".

Making the Stripe Blocks

Sew together three white 2½" × 10½" pieces and two different pink 2½" × 10½" pieces along the long edges to make a Stripe block. The block should measure 10½" square, including seam allowances. Make 17 Stripe blocks.

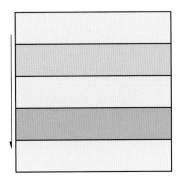

Make 17 blocks,
10½" × 10½".

Assembling the Quilt Top

1 Sew together three X blocks and two Stripe blocks to make a row as shown. Make four rows that measure 10½" × 50½", including seam allowances.

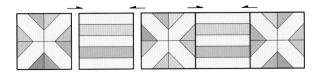

Make 4 rows,
10½" × 50½".

2 Sew together three Stripe blocks and two X blocks to make a row as shown. Make three rows that measure 10½" × 50½", including seam allowances.

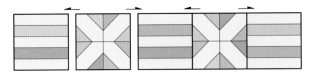

Make 3 rows,
10½" × 50½".

THE COLOR PINK

Pink symbolizes youth, playfulness, romance, and charm. It's a cheerful color that also conveys nurturing compassion and femininity. The phrase "in the pink" means in good health. The color is said to invoke kindness, sympathy, and calm. It seems the perfect color for a quilt, an item that brings warmth and comfort into our lives.

Pieced by Amber Johnson; quilted by Jen Ostler

FINISHED QUILT: 50½" × 70½" // **FINISHED BLOCK:** 10" × 10"

3 Sew the rows together as shown in the quilt
assembly diagram. The quilt top should measure
50½" × 70½".

Quilt assembly

Finishing the Quilt

Refer to "Finishing" on page 75 for details as needed.

1 Trim the selvages from the backing fabric and cut
it into two pieces, approximately 42" × 58" each.
With right sides together, join the pieces along the
long edges to make a backing with a horizontal seam.
Press the seam allowances to one side.

2 Layer the quilt top with batting and backing and
quilt as desired. The quilt shown is machine
quilted with the Compass Small pantograph by Patricia
E. Ritter and Leisha Farnsworth with an overall design
of elongated triangles that create the look of stars.

3 Use the pink 2½" × 20" strips to make scrappy
double-fold binding (see page 77). Attach the
binding to the quilt. Add a label, if desired.

Blossoms and Buds

This quilt would be so cute paired with some black-and-white Halloween quilts or cozy fall decor. Who would ever think that a quilt made only with orange and white would be so appealing?! I'm also dying to make a non-scrappy version with just two fabrics, replacing the orange with a navy blue print and keeping the white background. So if that's your preference, go for it!

Materials

Yardage is based on 42"-wide fabric.

6¼ yards *total* of assorted orange prints for blocks, setting squares, and setting triangles

1¾ yards of white solid for blocks

¾ yard of orange print for binding

5½ yards of fabric for backing

77" × 99" piece of batting

Cutting

All measurements include ¼" seam allowances.

From the assorted orange prints, cut a *total* of:
3 squares, 16" × 16"; cut into quarters diagonally to yield 12 triangles (2 are extra)
18 squares, 10½" × 10½"
4 squares, 10¼" × 10¼"; cut into quarters diagonally to yield 16 triangles (2 are extra)
2 squares, 8½" × 8½"; cut in half diagonally to yield 4 triangles
17 squares, 6½" × 6½"
384 squares, 2½" × 2½"

From the white solid, cut:
21 strips, 2½" × 42"; crosscut into 336 squares, 2½" × 2½"

From the orange print for binding, cut:
9 strips, 2½" × 42"

Making the Blocks

Press seam allowances in the directions indicated by the arrows.

Arrange eight orange 2½" squares and seven white squares in three rows as shown. Sew the squares together into rows. Sew the rows together to make a Checkerboard block that measures 6½" × 10½", including seam allowances. Make 48 blocks.

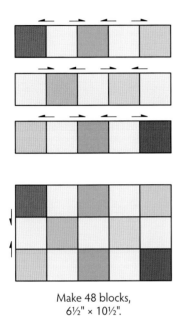

Make 48 blocks,
6½" × 10½".

Assembling the Quilt Top

1 Arrange the pieced blocks, the orange 10½" squares, the orange 6½" squares, and all of the orange setting triangles in diagonal rows as shown in the quilt assembly diagram on page 25. (Note that the setting triangles are cut oversized and will be trimmed later.) When you're happy with the placement, sew the blocks, squares, and side setting triangles together into rows. Trim the dog-ears after pressing.

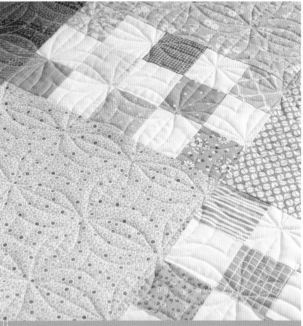

THE COLOR ORANGE

Orange exudes energy, warmth, confidence, and creativity. While commonly associated with the heat of summer, orange is also linked to autumn, bringing to mind pumpkins and the changing colors of the leaves. Orange is said to be an optimistic color, encouraging social communication and enthusiasm. In a quilt, it will definitely provide warmth and joy.

Pieced by Amber Johnson; quilted by Jen Ostler

FINISHED QUILT: 68½" × 91" // **FINISHED BLOCK: 6" × 10"**

2 Sew the rows together. Add the corner triangles last, centering them on the adjacent rows. Press the seam allowances toward the triangles and the rows with the orange 10½" squares.

3 Trim and square up the quilt top, leaving a ¼" seam allowance beyond the outer point of the Checkerboard blocks. The quilt should now measure approximately 68½" × 91".

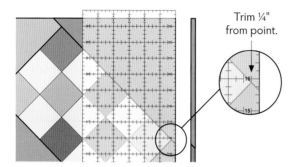

Trim ¼" from point.

Finishing the Quilt

Refer to "Finishing" on page 75 for details as needed.

1 Trim the selvages from the backing fabric and cut it into two pieces, approximately 42" × 99" each. With right sides together, join the pieces along the long edges to make a backing with a vertical seam. Press the seam allowances to one side.

2 Layer the quilt top with batting and backing and quilt as desired. The quilt shown is machine quilted with a design similar to an orange peel, a pantograph called Twinkle Toes by Karlee Porter.

3 Use the orange 2½"-wide strips to make double-fold binding and then attach the binding to the quilt. Add a label, if desired.

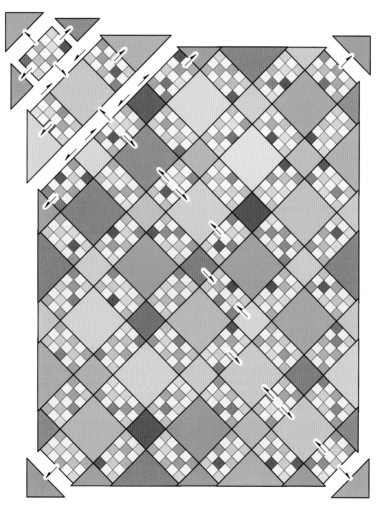

Quilt assembly

Crowning Glory

Greenish yellows can sometimes carry a negative connotation, but this yellow quilt is far from sickly. The bursts of yellow in this pattern exude happiness! I can envision this pattern in so many different colorways. Can you?

Materials

Yardage is based on 42"-wide fabric.

3½ yards *total* of assorted yellow prints for blocks and sashing

5 yards of white print for blocks, sashing, and border

⅔ yard of yellow stripe for binding

5⅛ yards of fabric for backing

74" × 92" piece of batting

Cutting

All measurements include ¼" seam allowances.

From the assorted yellow prints, cut a *total* of:

16 squares, 7⅜" × 7⅜"; cut into quarters diagonally to yield 64 triangles (2 are extra)

31 squares, 4¾" × 4¾"

48 squares, 4½" × 4½"

96 squares, 3" × 3"

From the white print, cut:

3 strips, 8½" × 42"; crosscut into 12 squares, 8½" × 8½"

7 strips, 7⅜" × 42"; crosscut into 31 squares, 7⅜" × 7⅜". Cut the squares into quarters diagonally to yield 124 triangles.

4 strips, 6½" × 42"; crosscut into 20 squares, 6½" × 6½"

16 strips, 3" × 42"; crosscut *8 of the strips* into 96 squares, 3" × 3"

3 strips, 2½" × 42"; crosscut into 48 squares, 2½" × 2½"

From the yellow stripe, cut:

8 strips, 2½" × 42"

Making the Blocks

Press seam allowances in the directions indicated by the arrows.

1 Draw a diagonal line from corner to corner on the wrong side of the white 3" squares. Or, use Diagonal Seam Tape (page 73) to avoid marking. Place a marked square on top of a yellow 3" square with right sides together. Pin the squares together and sew ¼" from both sides of the drawn line. Cut on the drawn line to yield two half-square-triangle units. Trim each unit to 2½" square. Make 192 units.

Make 192 units.

2 Draw a diagonal line from corner to corner on the wrong side of the yellow 4½" squares. Place a marked square on one corner of a white 8½" square with right sides together. Pin in place and sew on the drawn line. Trim ¼" from the stitching line. Repeat in each corner to make a block center that measures 8½" square, including seam allowances. Make 12 units.

Make 12 units, 8½" × 8½".

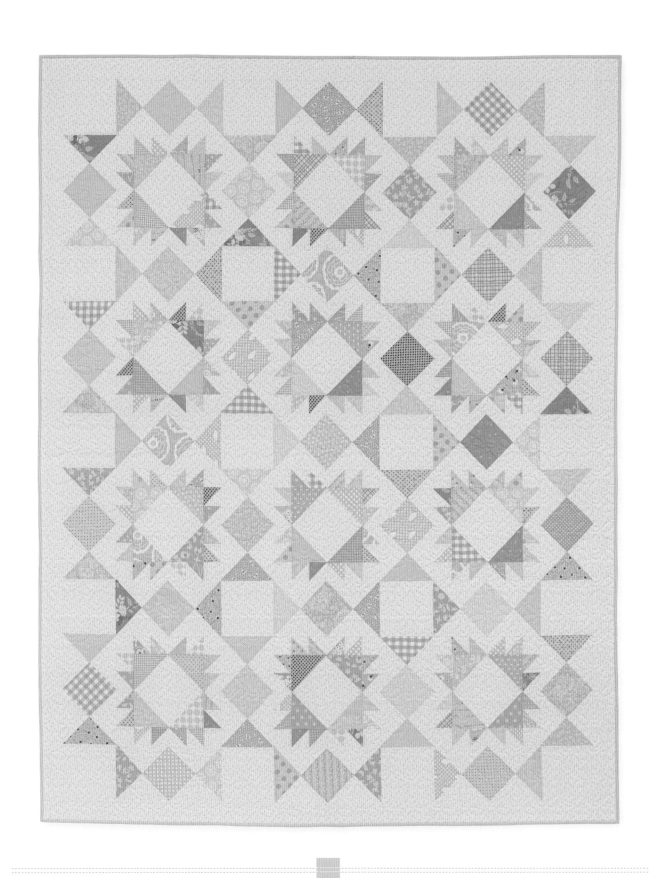

Pieced by Amber Johnson; quilted by Jen Ostler

FINISHED QUILT: 65½" × 83½" // **FINISHED BLOCK: 12" × 12"**

3 Sew together four half-square-triangle units from step 1 to make a row as shown. Make 48 rows that measure 2½" × 8½", including seam allowances.

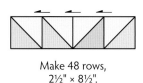

Make 48 rows,
2½" × 8½".

4 Sew a white 2½" square to each end of a row from step 3 to make a row that measures 2½" × 12½", including seam allowances. Make 24 rows.

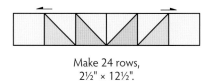

Make 24 rows,
2½" × 12½".

5 Arrange and sew together two rows from step 3, two rows from step 4, and a center unit from step 2, matching the center of each row with the points of the center unit, to make a Crown block that measures 12½" square, including seam allowances. Make 12 blocks.

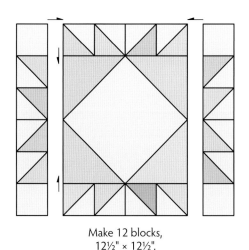

Make 12 blocks,
12½" × 12½".

THE COLOR YELLOW

The color yellow radiates happiness, light, joy, and optimism! Pure yellow represents sweet things like sunshine and lemons, as well as springtime and Easter. Verbs associated with the color include inspire, clarify, amuse, *and* energize. *On the flip side, it can also represent qualities of cowardice, egotism, and deceit. In quiltmaking, we'll stick with the notion of a cheerful, energetic color that provides happiness and brings joy to our lives.*

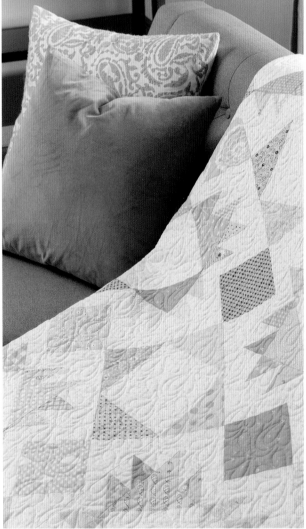

Making the Sashing Units

Arrange and sew two yellow triangles, one yellow 4¾" square, and four white triangles in diagonal rows as shown. Press and trim the dog-ears. Sew the rows together to make a sashing unit. Trim the unit to 6½" × 12½". Make 31 sashing units.

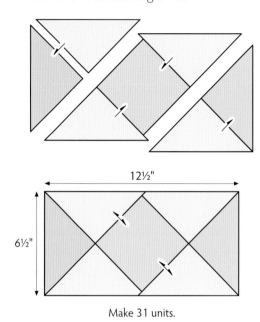

Make 31 units.

Assembling the Quilt Top

1 Arrange and sew four white 6½" squares and three sashing units into a row as shown. Make five sashing rows that measure 6½" × 60½", including seam allowances.

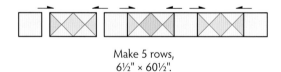

Make 5 rows,
6½" × 60½".

2 Arrange and sew four sashing units and three blocks into a row that measures 12½" × 60½", including seam allowances. Make four block rows.

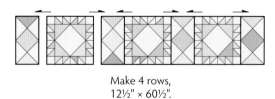

Make 4 rows,
12½" × 60½".

3 Sew together the rows from steps 1 and 2, referring to the quilt assembly diagram below. The quilt center should measure 60½" × 78½", including seam allowances.

4 Trim the selvages from the eight white 3" × 42" strips. Sew them together end to end with a straight seam to make one long strip. Press the seam allowances in one direction. From the pieced strip, cut two strips, 3" × 78½", and sew them to opposite sides of the quilt center. Cut two more strips, 3" × 65½", and sew them to the top and bottom. The quilt top should measure 65½" × 83½".

Finishing the Quilt

Refer to "Finishing" on page 75 for details as needed.

1 Trim the selvages from the backing fabric and cut it into two pieces, approximately 42" × 92" each. With right sides together, join the pieces along the long edges to make a backing with a vertical seam. Press the seam allowances to one side.

2 Layer the quilt top with batting and backing and quilt as desired. The quilt shown is machine quilted with an allover design of four feather-like loops with an echo, which is the Cassava pantograph by Sarah Ann Myers.

3 Use the yellow stripe 2½"-wide strips to make double-fold binding and then attach the binding to the quilt. Add a label, if desired.

Quilt assembly

Box Elder Trail

Green is a common "favorite color," second only to blue. It reminds me of the beautiful earth and all things fresh and alive! This quilt design features a super easy block. It's an opportunity to delve into your stash and create a fabulous homage to spring.

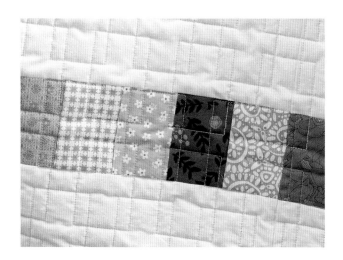

Materials

Yardage is based on 42"-wide fabric.

1⅝ yards *total* of assorted green prints for blocks

3 yards of beige tone on tone for blocks

⅝ yard of green print for binding

4 yards of fabric for backing

67" × 77" piece of batting

Cutting

All measurements include ¼" seam allowances.

From the assorted green prints, cut a *total* of:
210 pieces, 2½" × 3½"

From the beige tone on tone, cut:
9 strips, 10½" × 42"; crosscut into 84 pieces, 4" × 10½"

From the green print for binding, cut:
7 strips, 2½" × 42"

Making the Blocks

Press seam allowances in the directions indicated by the arrows.

1 Sew together five assorted green 2½" × 3½" pieces along the 3½" edges. The unit should measure 3½" × 10½", including seam allowances. Make 42 units.

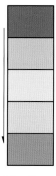

Make 42 units,
3½" × 10½".

2 Sew a beige 4" × 10½" piece to each long side of a green unit to make a block that measures 10½" square, including seam allowances. Make 42 blocks.

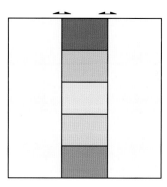

Make 42 blocks,
10½" × 10½".

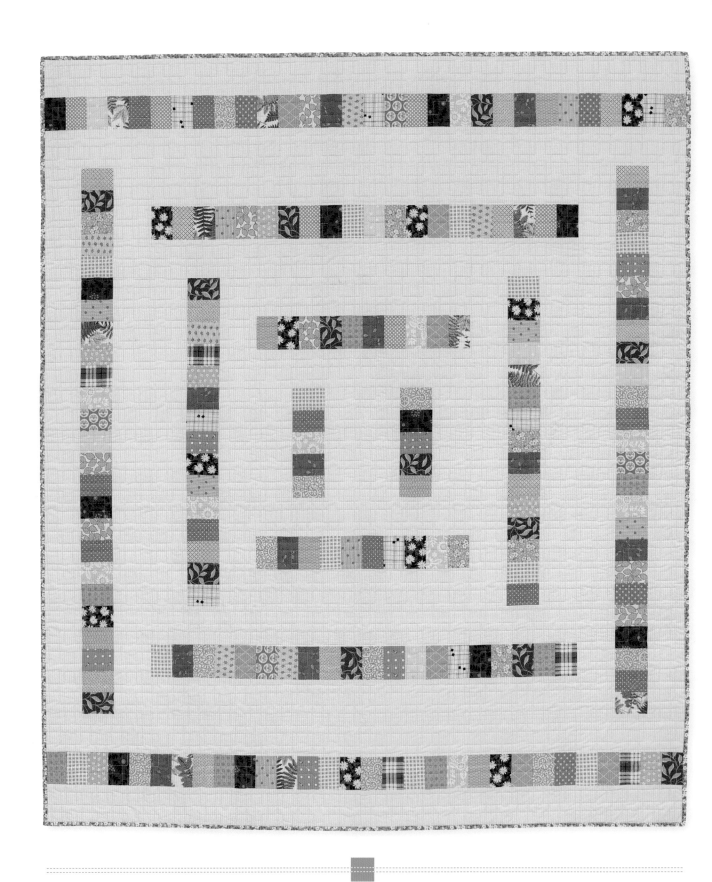

Pieced by Amber Johnson; quilted by Jen Ostler

FINISHED QUILT: 60½" × 70½" // **FINISHED BLOCK: 10" × 10"**

Assembling the Quilt Top

Arrange and sew the blocks into seven rows of six blocks each, rotating the blocks as shown in the quilt assembly diagram. Sew the rows together. The quilt should measure 60½" × 70½".

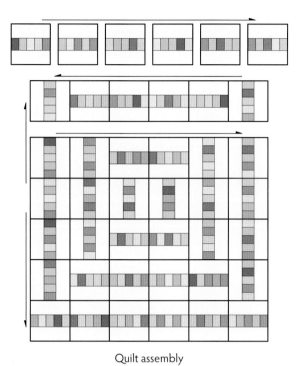

Quilt assembly

Finishing the Quilt

Refer to "Finishing" on page 75 for details as needed.

1 Trim the selvages from the backing fabric and cut it into two pieces, approximately 42" × 72" each. With right sides together, join the pieces along the long edges to make a backing with a horizontal seam. Press the seam allowances to one side.

2 Layer the quilt top with batting and backing and quilt as desired. The quilt shown is machine quilted using the Simple Squares pantograph by Brandon Smythe, with a slight tweaking of the design to create rectangles instead of squares.

3 Use the green 2½"-wide strips to make double-fold binding and then attach the binding to the quilt. Add a label, if desired.

THE COLOR GREEN

Green is the color of life, renewal, and growth. It is considered a relaxing color that re-energizes and balances our emotions. Sometimes it is used to symbolize jealousy, greed, or lack of experience. Quilters see green in terms of generosity, hope, luck, and prosperity. A quilt embodies the green notions of safety, security, harmony, and health.

Seaside

Teal is such a beautiful color, don't you think? I loved using it as a background in this quilt. It's the perfect balance of calm and happy! This is a rare situation in which the background is scrappier than the main design, enabling you to use up lots of similar-toned fabrics from your stash. All you need to add is a little bit of yardage in a contrasting color to bring them all together. Another option is to replace the teal solid with dark scraps of the same color.

Materials

Yardage is based on 42"-wide fabric.

5¼ yards *total* of assorted aqua prints for blocks and sashing

2½ yards of teal solid for blocks, sashing, and binding

5⅛ yards of fabric for backing

79" × 91" piece of batting

Cutting

All measurements include ¼" seam allowances.

From the assorted aqua prints, cut a *total* of:
30 pieces, 2½" × 12½"
30 pieces, 2½" × 10½"
72 pieces, 2½" × 8½"
72 pieces, 2½" × 6½"
72 pieces, 2½" × 4½"
72 squares, 2½" × 2½"

From the teal solid, cut:
12 strips, 4½" × 42"; crosscut into 180 pieces, 2½" × 4½"

10 strips, 2½" × 42"; crosscut *2 of the strips* into 25 squares, 2½" × 2½"

Making the Blocks

For a super scrappy look, use eight different aqua fabrics in each block. Press seam allowances in the directions indicated by the arrows.

1 Sew together one aqua 2½" × 8½" piece and one teal 2½" × 4½" piece end to end. Make 72 units that measure 2½" × 12½", including seam allowances.

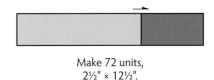

Make 72 units,
2½" × 12½".

2 Sew together one aqua 2½" × 6½" piece, one teal 2½" × 4½" piece, and one aqua 2½" square end to end to make a unit that measures 2½" × 12½", including seam allowances. Make 72 units.

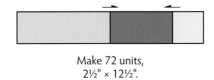

Make 72 units,
2½" × 12½".

3 Sew together two aqua 2½" × 4½" pieces and one teal 2½" × 4½" piece end to end to make a unit that measures 2½" × 12½", including seam allowances. Make 36 units.

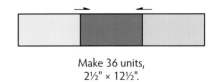

Make 36 units,
2½" × 12½".

Pieced by Amber Johnson; quilted by Jen Ostler

FINISHED QUILT: 70½" × 82½" // **FINISHED BLOCK: 10" × 12"**

4 Sew together two units from step 1, two units from step 2, and one unit from step 3 as shown to make an A block that measures 10½" × 12½", including seam allowances. Make 18 A blocks.

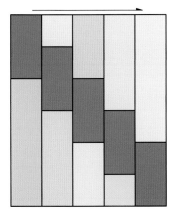

Make 18 A blocks,
10½" × 12½".

5 Sew together two units from step 1, two units from step 2, and one unit from step 3 as shown to make a B block that measures 10½" × 12½", including seam allowances. Make 18 B blocks.

Make 18 B blocks,
10½" × 12½".

THE COLOR AQUA

Aqua, which is sometimes referred to as cyan, sits between green and blue on the color wheel. It embodies sky and sea, symbolizing balance, serenity, stability, peace, growth, and energy. It is referred to as the color of calmness and clarity, and can increase empathy and compassion. Sounds like the perfect color for a quilt!

Assembling the Quilt Top

1 Sew together three A blocks, three B blocks, and five aqua 2½" × 12½" pieces to make a row as shown. The row should measure 12½" × 70½", including seam allowances. Make three rows.

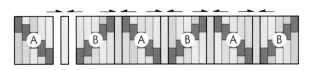

Make 3 rows,
12½" × 70½".

2 Sew together three A blocks, three B blocks, and five aqua 2½" × 12½" pieces to make a row as shown. The row should measure 12½" × 70½", including seam allowances. Make three rows.

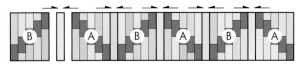

Make 3 rows,
12½" × 70½".

3 Sew together six aqua 2½" × 10½" pieces and five teal 2½" squares to make a sashing row as shown. The row should measure 2½" × 70½", including seam allowances. Make five rows.

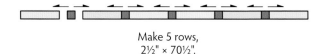

Make 5 rows,
2½" × 70½".

Fabric Choices Speak Volumes

This pattern would look beautiful made with "low-volume" fabrics (prints with a light background and a very subtle print) in place of the assorted aqua prints. Choose your favorite bold color for the accent pieces, or go for a variety of bold prints or solids for a rainbow effect!

4 Sew the block rows and sashing rows together as shown in the quilt assembly diagram below. The quilt top should measure 70½" × 82½".

Finishing the Quilt

Refer to "Finishing" on page 75 for details as needed.

1 Trim the selvages from the backing fabric and cut it into two pieces, approximately 42" × 92" each. With right sides together, join the pieces along the long edges to make a backing with a vertical seam. Press the seam allowances to one side.

2 Layer the quilt top with batting and backing and quilt as desired. The quilt shown is machine quilted with the Flower Child pantograph by Apricot Moon, creating a field of linked five-petal flowers.

3 Use the teal 2½"-wide strips to make double-fold binding and then attach the binding to the quilt. Add a label, if desired.

Quilt assembly

Patchwork Plaid

Blue has always been my favorite color and probably always will be. If you're like me and have more blue than anything else in your stash, pull out the blues and make this quilt! It features three different Plus Sign blocks that are oh-so-classic, just like the color combination of blue and white. I had hoped to whittle down my blue stash, but for some reason it just keeps growing!

Materials

Yardage is based on 42"-wide fabric.

2⅔ yards of white solid for A and C blocks

2 yards of navy print for A blocks and binding

3 yards *total* of assorted light to medium blue prints for B and C blocks (collectively referred to as "medium blue")

⅞ yard *total* of assorted dark blue to navy prints for B and C blocks (collectively referred to as "dark blue")

5½ yards of fabric for backing

79" × 99" piece of batting

Cutting

All measurements include ¼" seam allowances.

From the white solid, cut:

16 strips, 4½" × 42"; crosscut into 124 squares, 4½" × 4½"

5 strips, 2½" × 42"; crosscut into 80 squares, 2½" × 2½"

From the navy print, cut:

2 strips, 10½" × 42"; crosscut into 31 pieces, 2½" × 10½"

4 strips, 4½" × 42"; crosscut into 62 pieces, 2½" × 4½"

9 strips, 2½" × 42"

From the assorted medium blue prints, cut:

12 matching sets of:
    2 pieces, 2½" × 10½"
    2 pieces, 2½" × 6½"
    4 squares, 2½" × 2½"
20 matching sets of:
    4 pieces, 2½" × 6½"
    5 squares, 2½" × 2½"

From the assorted dark blue prints, cut:

12 matching sets of:
    1 piece, 2½" × 6½"
    2 squares, 2½" × 2½"
20 matching sets of 4 squares, 2½" × 2½"

Making the A Blocks

Use the pieces cut from the navy print yardage for the A blocks. Press seam allowances in the directions indicated by the arrows.

1 Sew together two white 4½" squares and one navy 2½" × 4½" piece as shown to make a unit that measures 4½" × 10½", including seam allowances. Make 62 units.

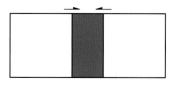

Make 62 units,
4½" × 10½".

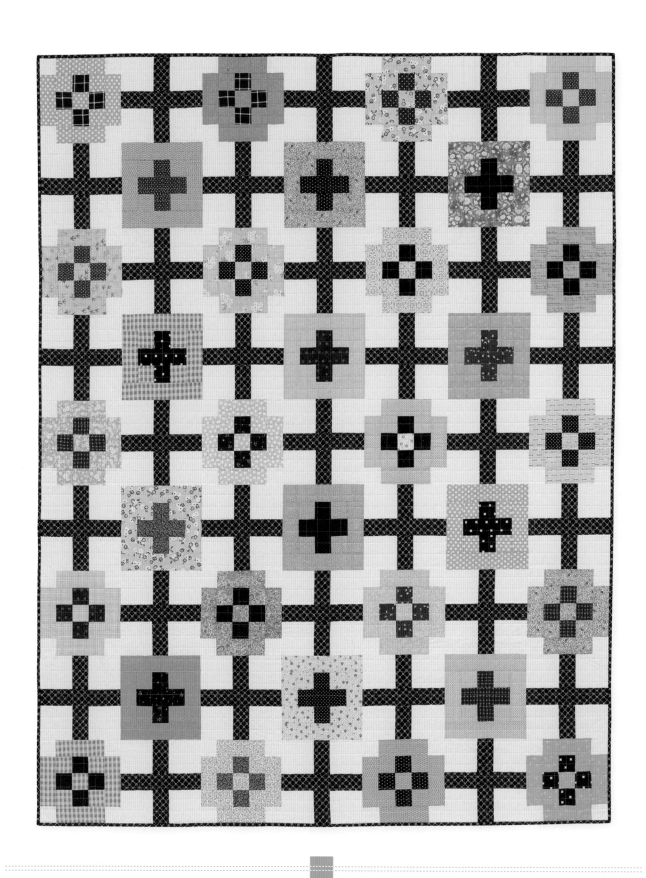

Pieced by Amber Johnson; quilted by Jen Ostler

FINISHED QUILT: 70½" × 90½" // **FINISHED BLOCK: 10" × 10"**

2 Sew two units from step 1 to one navy 2½" × 10½" piece to make an A block that measures 10½" square, including seam allowances. Make 31 A blocks.

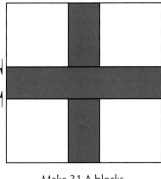

Make 31 A blocks,
10½" × 10½".

THE COLOR BLUE

Blue is timeless and tranquil; it symbolizes truth, trust, and loyalty. It has a calming and relaxing effect, promoting peace, honesty, security, and reliability. Sometimes it carries a touch of melancholy, as in the expression "feeling blue." However, research shows it is the favorite color of more people than any other. The positive obviously outweighs the negative. It's a lovely color. Think of the sky and the ocean!

Making the B Blocks

Use one dark blue print and one medium blue print for each block.

1 Join medium blue 2½" squares to opposite sides of a dark blue square. Make two units. Sew the units to opposite sides of a dark blue 2½" × 6½" piece to make a unit measuring 6½" square, including seam allowances.

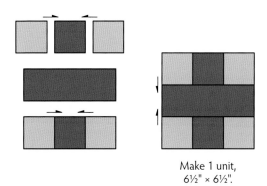

Make 1 unit,
6½" × 6½".

2 Sew medium blue 2½" × 6½" pieces to opposite sides of the step 1 unit. Sew medium blue 2½" × 10½" pieces to the top and bottom to make a B block that measures 10½" square, including seam allowances. Make 12 B blocks.

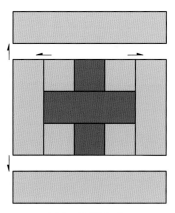

Make 12 B blocks,
10½" × 10½".

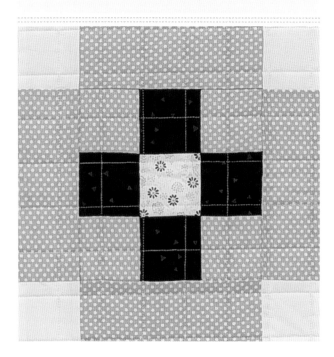

Make Do

Don't stress if you run out of a fabric and can't make completely matching sets of fabrics for the B or C blocks. I was just a tiny bit short on the medium blue prints used for this C block, so I supplemented with another fabric. I love the old-fashioned make-do feel it adds!

Making the C Blocks

Use one dark blue print and one medium blue print for each block.

1 Sew together four dark blue 2½" squares and five medium blue 2½" squares to make a nine-patch unit that measures 6½" square, including seam allowances.

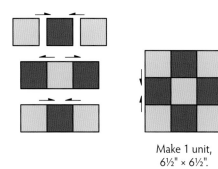

Make 1 unit,
6½" × 6½".

2 Arrange and sew four medium blue 2½" × 6½" pieces, four white 2½" squares, and a nine-patch unit into three rows as shown. Sew the rows together to make a C block that measures 10½" square, including seam allowances. Make 20 C blocks.

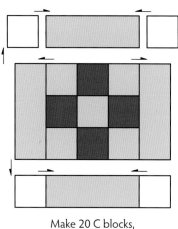

Make 20 C blocks,
10½" × 10½".

Assembling the Quilt Top

1 Sew together four C blocks and three A blocks to make a row. Make five rows that measure 10½" × 70½", including seam allowances.

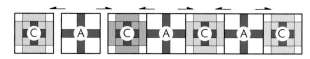

Make 5 rows,
10½" × 70½".

2 Sew together four A blocks and three B blocks to make a row. Make four rows that measure 10½" × 70½", including seam allowances.

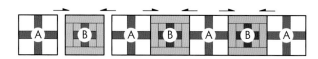

Make 4 rows,
10½" × 70½".

3 Sew the rows together in alternating positions, beginning and ending with the rows from step 1. The quilt top should measure 70½" × 90½".

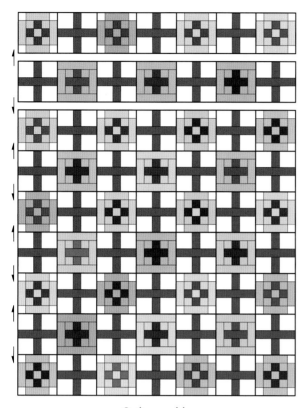

Quilt assembly

Finishing the Quilt

Refer to "Finishing" on page 75 for details as needed.

1 Trim the selvages from the backing fabric and cut it into two pieces, approximately 42" × 99" each. With right sides together, join the pieces along the long edges to make a backing with a vertical seam. Press the seam allowances to one side.

2 Layer the quilt top with batting and backing and quilt as desired. The quilt shown features machine quilting in a straight grid pattern.

3 Use the navy 2½"-wide strips to make double-fold binding and then attach the binding to the quilt. Add a label, if desired.

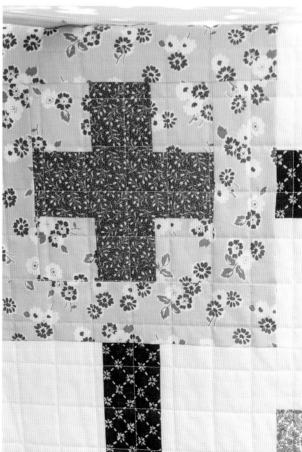

Glimmer of Light

Some of my favorite purples are the soft purples found in 1930s reproduction prints. The center star in this quilt is pieced from a reproduction print, while the outer star features a mix of both contemporary and vintage-looking prints to create an extra-scrappy look that I love. This star pattern is a classic and it's the perfect opportunity to get really scrappy in any colorway.

Materials

Yardage is based on 42"-wide fabric.

3¾ yards of white solid for blocks and background

1 yard of purple floral for center star and binding

1 yard *total* of assorted purple prints for outer star points

4 yards of fabric for backing

71" × 71" piece of batting

Cutting

All measurements include ¼" seam allowances.

From the white solid, cut:
2 strips, 16⅞" × 42"; crosscut into 4 squares, 16⅞" × 16⅞". Cut the squares in half diagonally to yield 8 triangles.

2 strips, 16½" × 42"; crosscut into 4 squares, 16½" × 16½"

2 strips, 8⅞" × 42"; crosscut into 8 squares, 8⅞" × 8⅞". Cut the squares in half diagonally to yield 16 triangles.

1 strip, 8½" × 42"; crosscut into 4 squares, 8½" × 8½"

1 strip, 5" × 42"; crosscut into 8 squares, 5" × 5"

1 strip, 4½" × 42"; crosscut into 8 squares, 4½" × 4½"

6 strips, 3" × 42"; crosscut into 72 squares, 3" × 3"

From the purple floral, cut:
1 strip, 5" × 42"; crosscut into 8 squares, 5" × 5"

1 strip, 4⅞" × 42"; crosscut into 8 squares, 4⅞" × 4⅞". Cut the squares in half diagonally to yield 16 triangles.

7 strips, 2½" × 42"

From the assorted purple prints, cut a *total* of:
72 squares, 3" × 3"

48 squares, 2⅞" × 2⅞"; cut in half diagonally to yield 96 triangles

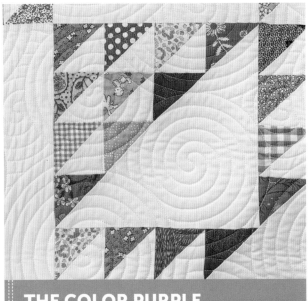

THE COLOR PURPLE

Purple is a mixture of red and blue. Because the dye was originally very expensive, the color has historically been associated with royalty or spirituality. It has symbolized power and strength, wisdom and creativity. Purple also is said to evoke a sense of peace, compassion, and sympathy.

Making the Center Star Blocks

Press seam allowances in the directions indicated by the arrows.

1 Draw a diagonal line from corner to corner on the wrong side of a white 5" square. Or, use Diagonal Seam Tape (page 73) to avoid marking. Place a marked square on top of a purple floral 5" square, right sides together. Pin the squares together and sew ¼" from both sides of the drawn line. Cut the squares on the drawn line to yield two half-square-triangle units. Trim each unit to 4½" square. Make 16 units.

Make 16 units.

2 Sew together two units from step 1 and two white 4½" squares in two rows as shown. Sew the rows together to make a unit that measures 8½" square, including seam allowances. Make four units.

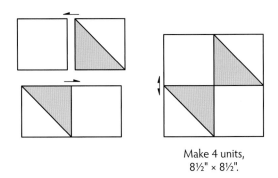

Make 4 units,
8½" × 8½".

3 Sew purple floral triangles to the white edges of a half-square-triangle unit from step 1. Trim the dog-ears. Make eight units.

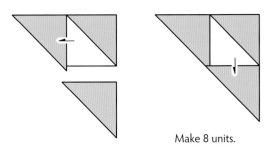

Make 8 units.

4 Sew together a unit from step 3 and a white 8⅞" triangle along the long edges. Trim the dog-ears. The unit should measure 8½" square, including seam allowances. Make eight units.

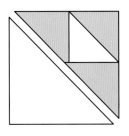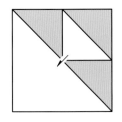

Make 8 units,
8½" × 8½".

5 Sew together two units from step 4, one unit from step 2, and one white 8½" square in two rows. Sew the rows together to make a center block that measures 16½" square, including seam allowances. Make four blocks.

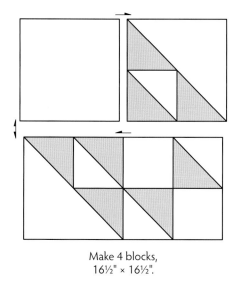

Make 4 blocks,
16½" × 16½".

Making the Outer Star Point Blocks

1 Draw a diagonal line from corner to corner on the wrong side of a white 3" square. Place a marked square on top of a purple print 3" square, right sides together. Pin the squares together and sew ¼" from both sides of the drawn line. Cut the squares on the drawn line to yield two half-square-triangle units. Trim each unit to 2½" square. Make 144 units.

Make 144 units.

Pieced by Amber Johnson; quilted by Jen Ostler

FINISHED QUILT: 64½" × 64½" // **FINISHED BLOCK: 16" × 16"**

2 Sew together six half-square-triangle units and four purple print triangles in rows as shown. Press and trim the dog-ears. Sew the rows together to make a pieced triangle. Press and trim the dog-ears. Make 24 pieced triangles.

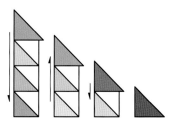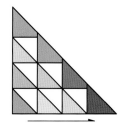

Make 24 units.

3 Sew together a pieced triangle from step 2 and a white 8⅞" triangle. Make eight units that measure 8½" square, including seam allowances.

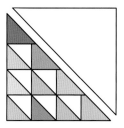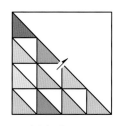

Make 8 units,
8½" × 8½".

4 Sew pieced triangles from step 2 to the white edges of a unit from step 3. Press and trim the dog-ears. Make eight units.

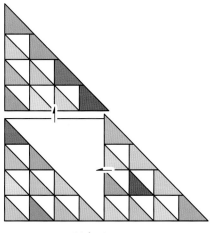

Make 8 units.

5 Sew together a unit from step 4 and a white 16⅞" triangle to make an outer block that measures 16½" square, including seam allowances. Make eight blocks.

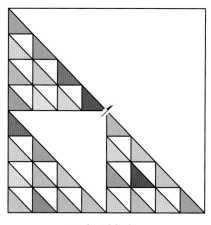

Make 8 blocks,
16½" × 16½".

Assembling the Quilt Top

1 Sew together two white 16½" squares and two outer blocks as shown. Make two rows that measure 16½" × 64½", including seam allowances.

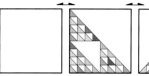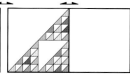

Make 2 rows,
16½" × 64½".

2 Sew together two outer blocks and two center blocks as shown. Make two rows that measure 16½" × 64½", including seam allowances.

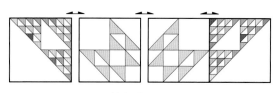

Make 2 rows,
16½" × 64½".

3 Sew the rows together as shown in the quilt assembly diagram below. The quilt top should measure 64½" square.

Finishing the Quilt

Refer to "Finishing" on page 75 for details as needed.

1 Trim the selvages from the backing fabric and cut it into two pieces, approximately 42" × 72" each. With right sides together, join the pieces along the long edges to make a backing with a vertical seam. Press the seam allowances to one side.

2 Layer the quilt top with batting and backing and quilt as desired. The quilt shown is machine quilted with the Raindrops on Water pantograph by Allison Payette.

3 Use the purple floral 2½"-wide strips to make double-fold binding and then attach the binding to the quilt. Add a label, if desired.

Quilt assembly

Tile Revival

There is something about this sweet, delicate pattern paired with a variety of black prints and a white print background that creates whimsy and a sense of balance. Pull out your stash of black prints and have some dark fun! Or, keep an open mind and consider other options among your scraps—the quilt would be just as captivating in any colorway.

Materials

Yardage is based on 42"-wide fabric.

3⅓ yards of white print for blocks

1⅝ yards *total* of assorted black prints for blocks

⅝ yard of black solid for blocks

⅝ yard of black print for binding

3⅝ yards of fabric for backing*

63" × 71" piece of batting

*The featured quilt has a fun scrappy backing. See the photo on page 61 and "Making a Scrappy Quilt Back" on page 76 for additional details.

Cutting

All measurements include ¼" seam allowances.

From the white print, cut:
9 strips, 3¼" × 42"; crosscut into 105 squares, 3¼" × 3¼". Cut the squares into quarters diagonally to yield 420 triangles (2 are extra).
2 strips, 2⅞" × 42"; crosscut into 15 squares, 2⅞" × 2⅞". Cut the squares in half diagonally to yield 30 triangles.
29 strips, 2½" × 42"; crosscut into:
    224 pieces, 2½" × 3½"
    224 pieces, 1½" × 2½"

From the assorted black prints, cut:
56 matching sets of:
    1 square, 4½" × 4½"
    1 square, 3¼" × 3¼"; cut into quarters diagonally to yield 4 triangles

From the black solid, cut:
5 strips, 3¼" × 42"; crosscut into 49 squares, 3¼" × 3¼". Cut the squares into quarters diagonally to yield 196 triangles (2 are extra).

From the black print for binding, cut:
7 strips, 2½" × 42"

THE COLOR BLACK

Black exudes drama, sophistication, and mystery. It has a formality to it (think tuxedos) and is also associated with death and mourning. Black is a strong, authoritative color that offers feelings of security and protection as well as elegance. Black is modern, yet classic and timeless.

Making the Center Blocks

Use matching black print pieces for each block. Press seam allowances in the directions indicated by the arrows.

1 Sew together two white 3¼" triangles, one black solid triangle, and one black print triangle as shown to make an A hourglass unit that measures 2½" square, including seam allowances. Make four A units.

Make 4 A units,
2½" × 2½".

2 Sew white 1½" × 2½" pieces to the sides of two A units to make two units that measure 2½" × 4½", including seam allowances.

Make 2 units,
2½" × 4½".

3 Arrange and sew two A hourglass units, two units from step 2, one matching black print 4½" square, and four white 2½" × 3½" pieces into three rows as shown. Sew the rows together to make a block that measures 8½" square, including seam allowances. Make 30 blocks.

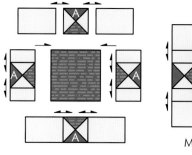 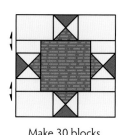

Make 30 blocks,
8½" × 8½".

Making the Outer Blocks

The outer blocks consist of four blocks for the corners and 22 blocks for the sides, top, and bottom edges of the quilt. As with the center blocks, use matching black print pieces for each outer block.

1 Sew together one black print triangle and one white 3¼" triangle along the short sides as shown. Make four B units.

Make 4 B units.

2 Repeat step 1 to sew together one black solid triangle and one white 3¼" triangle. Make two C units.

Make 2 C units.

3 Sew together a B unit and a white 2⅞" triangle along the long edges as shown to make a D unit that measures 2½" square, including seam allowances. Make two. Sew the remaining two B units to the C units to make two E hourglass units that measure 2½" square, including seam allowances.

Make 2 D units,   Make 2 E units,
2½" × 2½".   2½" × 2½".

4 Sew white 1½" × 2½" pieces to the sides of one D and one E unit as shown to make units that measure 2½" × 4½", including seam allowances.

Make 1 of each unit,
2½" × 4½".

5 Arrange and sew four white 2½" × 3½" pieces, the D and E units, the units from step 4, and a matching black print 4½" square together in three rows as shown. Sew the rows together to make a corner block that measures 8½" square, including seam allowances. Make two of these corner blocks.

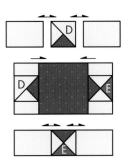 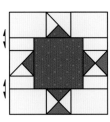

Make 2 corner blocks,
8½" × 8½".

6 Repeat steps 1–5 to make two more corner blocks as shown.

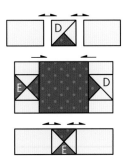 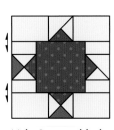

Make 2 corner blocks,
8½" × 8½".

7 For the remaining outer blocks, repeat steps 1–5, but in step 2, make three C units. In step 3, make one D unit and three E hourglass units. You need just one D unit for each of the blocks along the outer edges of the quilt.

Make 3 C units.

Make 1 D unit,   Make 3 E units,
2½" × 2½".   2½" × 2½".

8 Make a total of 22 outer blocks as shown: 10 blocks for the top and bottom, 6 blocks for the left side, and 6 blocks for the right side. The result is blocks in which the background pieces are all going in the same direction.

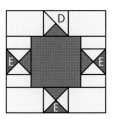

Make 10 blocks for top/bottom rows,
8½" × 8½".

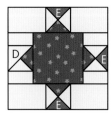 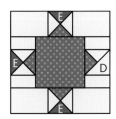

Make 6 blocks for   Make 6 blocks for
outer left edge,   outer right edge,
8½" × 8½".   8½" × 8½".

Pieced by Amber Johnson; quilted by Jen Ostler

FINISHED QUILT: 56½" × 64½" // **FINISHED BLOCK: 8" × 8"**

Assembling the Quilt Top

Arrange the outer and center blocks in rows as shown in the quilt assembly diagram below. Be sure to keep the blocks oriented so that the white rectangles are all positioned horizontally. Additionally, make sure the corner, top/bottom row blocks, left side, and right side blocks are positioned correctly. You should only have white pieces around the perimeter of the quilt. Sew the blocks together in horizontal rows. Sew the rows together. The quilt top should measure 56½" × 64½".

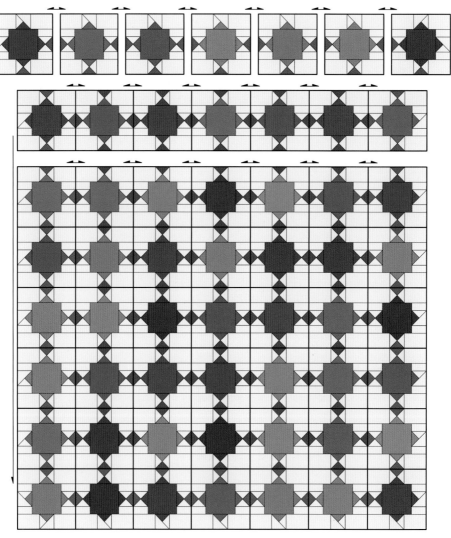

Quilt assembly

Finishing the Quilt

Refer to "Finishing" on page 75 for details as needed.

1 Trim the selvages from the backing fabric and cut it into two pieces, approximately 42" × 65" each. With right sides together, join the pieces along the long edges to make a backing with a horizontal seam. Press the seam allowances to one side.

2 Layer the quilt top with batting and backing and quilt as desired. The quilt shown is machine quilted with Modern Twist, an edge-to-edge pattern of vertical loops by Patricia E. Ritter.

3 Use the black print 2½"-wide strips to make double-fold binding and then attach the binding to the quilt. Add a label, if desired.

Making a scrappy backing is a great way to use random pieces of fabric from your stash. See page 76 for additional information.

Star Studded

The inspiration for this quilt came from one of my Instagram followers who shared a photo of an antique quilt pieced in red and white, hoping that I would re-create it. It's a lovely, classic design, and I had fun putting my own spin on it with the ombré effect using soft, muted rainbow colors.

Materials

Yardage is based on 42"-wide fabric. Fat quarters measure 18" × 21"; fat eighths measure 9" × 21".

4¼ yards of cream solid for background

1 fat eighth of red polka dot for blocks (color 1)

1 fat quarter of hot pink floral for blocks (color 2)

1 fat quarter of coral print for blocks (color 3)

⅜ yard of gold floral for blocks (color 4)

½ yard of green floral for blocks (color 5)

⅝ yard of aqua plaid for blocks (color 6)

⅝ yard of teal floral for blocks (color 7)

½ yard of blue floral for blocks (color 8)

⅜ yard of periwinkle floral for blocks (color 9)

1 fat quarter of purple floral for blocks (color 10)

1 fat quarter of lavender floral for blocks (color 11)

1 fat eighth of pink floral for blocks (color 12)

⅝ yard of yellow print for binding

4¾ yards of fabric for backing

75" × 85" piece of batting

Note: It's helpful to number your fabrics, especially if you choose different colors for the diagonal rows of stars. This will make it easier to piece the various units needed for the quilt. Color numbers begin at the upper left with 1 and continue to the lower right with 12.

Cutting

All measurements include ¼" seam allowances.

From the cream solid, cut:
10 strips, 2½" × 42"; crosscut into 150 squares,
 2½" × 2½"
17 strips, 6½" × 42"; crosscut into:
 26 squares, 6½" × 6½"
 97 pieces, 4½" × 6½"

From *each* of the red polka dot and pink floral
(colors 1 and 12), cut:
1 square, 4½" × 4½"
8 squares, 2½" × 2½"

From *each* of the hot pink and lavender florals
(colors 2 and 11), cut:
2 squares, 4½" × 4½"
20 squares, 2½" × 2½"

From *each* of the coral print and purple floral
(colors 3 and 10), cut:
3 squares, 4½" × 4½"
32 squares, 2½" × 2½"

From *each* of the gold and periwinkle florals
(colors 4 and 9), cut:
4 squares, 4½" × 4½"
44 squares, 2½" × 2½"

From *each* of the green and blue florals
(colors 5 and 8), cut:
5 squares, 4½" × 4½"
56 squares, 2½" × 2½"

Continued on page 65

Pieced by Amber Johnson; quilted by Jen Ostler

FINISHED QUILT: 66½" × 76½" // **FINISHED BLOCK: 6" × 6"**

Continued from page 62

From *each* of the aqua plaid and teal floral (colors 6 and 7), cut:

6 squares, 4½" × 4½"

68 squares, 2½" × 2½"

From the yellow print for binding, cut:

8 strips, 2½" × 42"

Making the Nine Patch Blocks

Press seam allowances in the directions indicated by the arrows.

1 Arrange and sew four hot pink 2½" squares (color 2) and five cream 2½" squares into three rows as shown. Sew the rows together to make a Nine Patch block that measures 6½" square, including seam allowances.

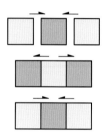 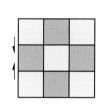

Color 2: make 1 block,
6½" × 6½".

2 Repeat step 1 to make Nine Patch blocks in the colors and quantities shown.

Make 1 block,
6½" × 6½".

Make 2 of each block,
6½" × 6½".

Make 3 of each block,
6½" × 6½".

Make 4 of each block,
6½" × 6½".

Make 5 of each block,
6½" × 6½".

Making the Star-Point Units

1 Draw a diagonal line from corner to corner on the wrong side of the remaining 2½" squares. Or, use Diagonal Seam Tape (page 73) to avoid marking.

2 Place a red polka dot square (color 1) on one corner of a cream 4½" × 6½" piece with right sides together as shown. Pin the pieces together and stitch on the drawn line. Trim ¼" from the stitching line. Repeat with a second red polka dot square in the adjacent corner to make an outer star-point unit that measures 4½" × 6½", including seam allowances. Make two units.

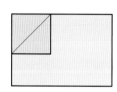 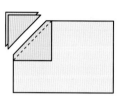

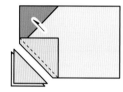 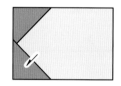

Color 1: make 2 units,
4½" × 6½".

3 Repeat step 2 to make outer star-point units in the colors and quantities shown—two each of all except aqua and teal (colors 6 and 7); make three each of those two colors.

Make 2 of each unit,
4½" × 6½".

Make 2 of each unit,
4½" × 6½".

Make 3 of each unit,
4½" × 6½".

4 Place a red polka dot 2½" square (color 1) on one corner of a cream 4½" × 6½" piece and place a hot pink 2½" square on the opposite corner. Sew and trim as before. Repeat in the remaining two corners as shown so that the red triangles are on the left end and the hot pink triangles are on the right end, making an inner star-point unit that measures 4½" × 6½", including seam allowances. Make two units.

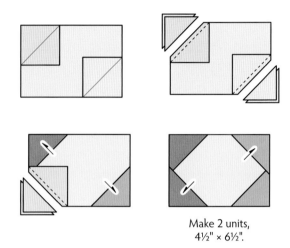

Make 2 units, 4½" × 6½".

5 Repeat step 4 to make inner star-point units in the colors and quantities shown.

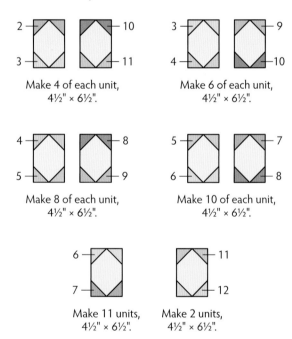

Make 4 of each unit, 4½" × 6½".

Make 6 of each unit, 4½" × 6½".

Make 8 of each unit, 4½" × 6½".

Make 10 of each unit, 4½" × 6½".

Make 11 units, 4½" × 6½".

Make 2 units, 4½" × 6½".

THE RAINBOW

A rainbow is composed of seven colors: red, orange, yellow, green, blue, indigo, and violet. It is a symbol of hope, promise, good luck, new beginnings, peace, tranquility, pride, and equality. There's something positive for everyone. Rainbow quilts don't have to feature bright, true colors. Try using muted or pastel versions of the typical rainbow hues for a more sophisticated look.

Assembling the Quilt Top

Lay out the cream 6½" squares, the star-point units, the Nine Patch blocks, and the various 4½" cream squares in rows as shown in the quilt assembly diagram below. Sew the blocks together in horizontal rows and then sew the rows together. The quilt top should measure 66½" × 76½".

Numbered Pins to the Rescue

To keep your pieces in order when sewing the rows, label the start of each row with a numbered pin (I love Marilee's Numbered Pins that come in a box of 130 pins numbered 1-20), or use a piece of paper. Then use the spiderweb piecing technique on page 74 to sew the pieces and rows in order.

Finishing the Quilt

Refer to "Finishing" on page 75 for details as needed.

1 Trim the selvages from the backing fabric and cut it into two pieces, approximately 42" × 85" each. With right sides together, join the pieces along the long edges to make a backing with a vertical seam. Press the seam allowances to one side.

2 Layer the quilt top with batting and backing and quilt as desired. The quilt shown is machine quilted with a Baptist Fan design by Allison Payette of Three Sisters Quilt.

3 Use the yellow 2½"-wide strips to make double-fold binding and then attach the binding to the quilt. Add a label, if desired.

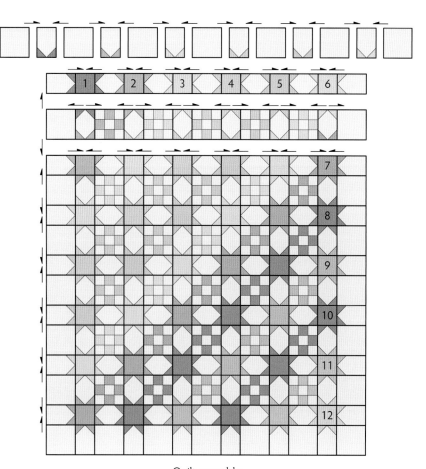

Quilt assembly

Quiltmaking Basics

Regardless of how long you've been quilting, there's always something new to learn and new tools to discover. And it's always a good idea to double-check to make sure your seam allowance is accurate before you begin a new project.

Tools and Supplies

Here's a list of necessary tools and some of my favorite, but not essential, accessories.

Self-healing cutting mat. Cutting mats come in different sizes and colors. Some even rotate! My favorite size is the 24" × 36" rectangular mat. It's the one that I always keep on my cutting table, and it's the perfect size for cutting across the width of fabric. My little 8" square rotating mat is another favorite when I'm cutting small pieces or trimming corners. Something in between those sizes is great for retreats or sewing days away from home. I have several different sizes on hand. Find the mat that fits your space, project, and budget.

Clear acrylic rulers. Rulers are available in many different shapes and sizes. The sizes I use the most are 6½" × 24" and 6½" square. I don't like to use rulers that are a lot bigger than the specific size piece I'm cutting; they can get a bit cumbersome and waste time. Rulers can be pricey, so I often look for coupons when treating myself to a new ruler. Having the right one definitely makes the cutting process easier and faster.

Rotary cutter, scissors, and seam ripper. A rotary cutter is essential for accurate cutting. Always keep extra blades on hand. Change the blade from time to time, especially if it starts skipping or requires more pressure to make a clean cut. Be very careful when handling the rotary cutter and blades so that you don't cut yourself—they're very sharp! Get into the habit of immediately closing the blade after cutting. Keep a pair of small embroidery scissors and a good seam ripper by your sewing machine for cutting threads and fixing mistakes. Large scissors for both fabric and paper are also good to have nearby.

Thread. Use threads of high quality (just like your fabric) to stand the test of time. There are several wonderful brands available, but I prefer Gutermann 100% cotton thread. Keep several neutral-colored spools on hand. Most often I use cream, but I always keep white and black in my inventory as well.

Sewing machine. I don't think you need a fancy sewing machine. In fact, all you really need is a machine that does a straight stitch; every other feature and stitch beyond that is a bonus! However, a good-quality machine is a must. Constantly dealing with issues such as wrong tension or thread breakage can be frustrating and take the joy out of sewing. Many wonderful brands are available in many different price ranges. I love my Bernina Quilter's Edition 550. Sewing-machine experts recommend having your machine serviced once every 12 to 18 months, depending on how much sewing you do.

Needles and straight pins. I typically use universal 70/10 needles in my sewing machine. Replace your needles regularly, such as at the beginning of every project. Keep a good supply of hand-sewing needles and straight pins, as well. Toss them when they become dull, bent, or burred.

Marking tools. Whether I'm drawing diagonal sewing lines for half-square-triangle units or marking the end of my binding, I like to use a Pilot FriXion erasable gel pen to mark fabric. The marks disappear with the touch of an iron. I use it only on parts of my fabric that won't ultimately be seen, *just in case* the ink happens to reappear.

Quilt labels. I often label my creations using customizable quilt labels that I purchase from online stores. You can usually select the size, font, text, and extra little details to make it your own. It's important to include the maker's name, the year the quilt was made, and the name of the quilt pattern. If there's room, you could also include the city and state of the maker as well as the recipient's name and occasion if the quilt is a gift. I've been buying simple labels from EverEmblem, an Etsy shop online, but you can also purchase them at your favorite quilt shop. Or make your own using fabric markers or embroidery, being as creative as you like.

Right or Wrong

Most print fabrics have two different sides. The front side of fabric, the side you want to see in the finished quilt, is the right side. The wrong side, or the back, is lighter. When piecing, always sew with the fabrics right sides together (sometimes abbreviated as "RST") unless instructed otherwise.

Techniques

Mastering the simple techniques below will help ensure that your pieces go together with ease, that your blocks are the correct size, and that the final quilt is flat and square. Take great care in both cutting and piecing. Accuracy is key!

ROTARY CUTTING

Most quilting instructions begin with cutting strips from selvage to selvage. This is the *width of the fabric* and is approximately 40" to 44". The easiest way to cut it is to keep your yardage folded. You can cut through a few layers at a time if you're careful. A 6½" × 24" or 6" × 24" ruler is best for cutting strips.

Square up one cut side of the fabric, cutting it at a 90° angle to the fold. Then, with the cut edge on your left (on your right if you are left-handed), place your ruler on the cut edge, aligning the desired dimension with the cut edge. Align a horizontal line along the fold, and cut along the edge of the ruler with your rotary cutter, keeping the ruler in position with your non-cutting hand. Continue cutting strips, making sure the cut edge of fabric and the appropriate markings are aligned. You may have to square up the cut end of fabric again after several cuts.

If you're cutting strips that are wider than your ruler, line up your fabric with the grid marks of your cutting mat and use them as guides.

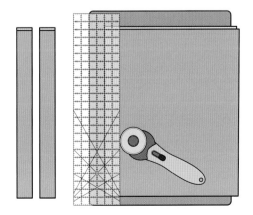

To cut squares or rectangles, first cut strips in the appropriate width. Then use a smaller square ruler, if you have one, to crosscut the strips into the desired pieces, aligning the marks of your ruler with the fabric.

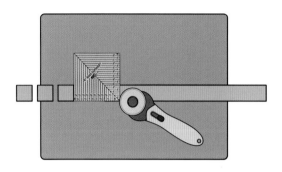

PIECING A PERFECT SEAM

The standard seam allowance in quilting is ¼". There's no need to backstitch at the beginning and end of each seam (as you would in garment sewing), because every seam in quiltmaking is crossed over by another seam, securing the stitches in place.

Be sure you know where the correct ¼" mark is on your machine. It's always a good idea to do an accuracy test any time you're at a new machine or using a new presser foot, because every machine and presser foot is different. Try lining up a folded scrap of fabric where you believe the ¼" mark is. Sew a line and then measure from the edge of your fabric to the stitching line. If it is exactly ¼", you're good to go! If it's a little shaky, then practice, practice, practice until you're comfortable sewing an accurate ¼" seam allowance.

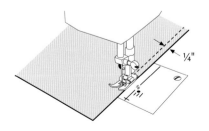

Piecing Time-Savers

Chain piecing *saves time and thread. Sew multiple units of fabric together one after the other in a chain, without clipping threads between each unit. Use small scissors or Stringblades (more on those shortly) to clip all the threads afterward.*

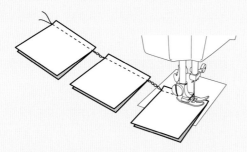

Spiderweb piecing *is a method of chain piecing units or blocks together in rows. It saves time and helps keep everything in order. Every unit/block/ row is connected with threads until you are ready to sew the rows together; then you clip the threads, press, and sew the rows together. I use this technique whenever possible, usually when I sew blocks together to assemble a quilt top. See "Spiderweb Piecing" on page 74 for additional details.*

Stringblades *are handy little thread cutters consisting of a blade that is surrounded by plastic. You can stick one to your table or sewing machine. I always keep one on the front of my machine to cut the threads between chain-pieced patches. They're very handy and a great time-saver! They're also removable so that you can replace them as needed. Stringblades are sold by Heather Andrus of Quilt Story.*

Diagonal Seam Tape *is washi tape that adheres to the front plate and table of your sewing machine to act as a guide when sewing seams on the diagonal. It's a great time-saving item, as you don't have to mark diagonal lines prior to stitching. Diagonal Seam Tape is sold by Allison Harris of Cluck, Cluck, Sew. See "Using Diagonal Seam Tape" on page 73 for further details.*

PRESSING

Pressing is a simple task, but it plays a big role in maintaining accuracy and in how easily your quilts go together. Press every seam before it's crossed by another seam to ensure that your blocks are straight and lie flat. Use a hot, dry iron (no steam) and take care not to stretch or pull on your fabric. Check both sides of your fabric after pressing. Make sure the fabric pieces don't overlap each other on the front. On the back, the seam allowances should lie flat and to one side (or open, if indicated in the project instructions).

Typically, you will press seam allowances toward the darker fabric or toward the piece that has fewer seams. If both pieces have a seam or two in them, I press the seam allowances open so that each piece will lie flat. Most projects will indicate the direction in which seam allowances should be pressed. Ideally, adjacent seam allowances will lie in opposing directions for easy matching and less bulk at seam intersections.

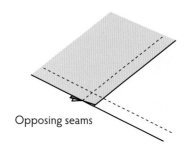

Opposing seams

Dog-Ears

Sometimes after piecing and pressing, little triangles of fabric extend beyond the main part of a unit, block, or quilt top. These are often referred to as "dog-ears" and should be trimmed.

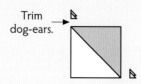

Trim dog-ears.

PINNING

If your cutting and seam allowances are accurate, and you have pressed carefully, most seam allowances should "nest" together. You shouldn't have to pin very often. However, pinning seam allowances at intersections can be helpful if you're having difficulty getting things to match up.

1 Make sure the seam allowances touch but do not overlap. Use your thumb and middle finger to wiggle the seam allowances right up to each other.

2 At the raw edge of your fabric, insert a pin on one side of the seam allowance and push it out through the other side of the stitches. Insert the pin on the side that will be farthest from your needle when sewing.

3 Sew the seam, right up to the pin. Keep the pin in place to secure the intersection until you've stitched it. Stop sewing, remove the pin, and then continue sewing. Be very careful not to sew over pins, as this can bend the pins, break a needle, and possibly even throw your machine's timing out of whack.

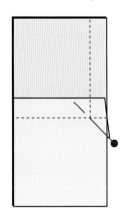

USING DIAGONAL SEAM TAPE

Cut a piece of Diagonal Seam Tape to adhere to your sewing machine. The longer the piece of tape is, the longer the diagonal line you can sew. Align the red line of the tape with your sewing-machine needle in the center needle position and press in place directly in front of the feed dogs, continuing onto the top of your sewing machine to the edge of the machine or sewing table. Make sure the tape is straight.

As an example, assume that you're sewing a square, layered right sides together with a rectangle, to make a flying-geese unit. Align the corners of the square so that opposite corners are on the red line of the tape. Stitch across the layered fabric, keeping the lower corners of the two pieces on the red line of tape the entire time. This technique saves time because you don't have to mark diagonal lines on the wrong side of your fabric for half-square-triangle units, flying-geese units, Snowball blocks, and more. See the product website, CluckCluckSewShop.com/products, and search for "diagonal seam tape" for more details.

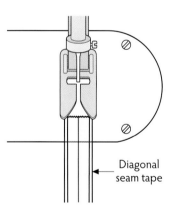

Diagonal
seam tape

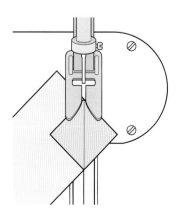

SPIDERWEB PIECING

I often use this method of chain piecing to sew all of my finished blocks together into rows. It keeps everything in order, saves time, and conserves thread. You can even do it to sew block units together.

1 Arrange the blocks (or block pieces) according to the quilt assembly diagram. When you are happy with the arrangement, start with the top row of blocks to be sewn together. Place them into a stack, beginning with the first block on the left and moving to the right. Keep the first block on top and place each of the blocks underneath the previous block in that row.

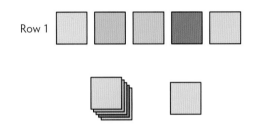

2 Repeat step 1 for each row, placing each stack below the top row in correct order.

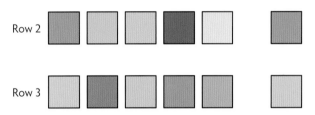

3 Move the stacks of blocks next to your sewing machine so that you can reach them while sewing. I find I can only do a handful of rows at a time, depending on how big my blocks are. Keep the stacks in the same order as they were in step 2.

4 Sew the first two blocks from row 1, stack 1, right sides together. (Sew all blocks right sides together.) Without clipping the thread (using chain piecing), sew the first two blocks from row 2, stack 2. Continue chain piecing the first two blocks from each row/stack. After sewing the first two blocks from the last row, clip the thread so that you can remove the entire length of chain-pieced blocks from under your presser foot. Do not clip the threads between each of the chain-pieced rows. You want them to stay connected.

5 Open up the first pair of chain-pieced blocks from step 4. Take the top block from stack 1 and sew it, using the chain-piecing method, onto the right end of the first pair of chain-pieced blocks in row 1. This should be the right edge of the second block in the first row. Continue to take the top block from each stack and sew it to the right edge of the second block in each row. Once you have finished sewing all of the top blocks from each stack, clip the final threads to remove the "spiderweb" of blocks from the machine. Keep all of the threads between the rows connected.

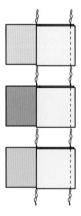

6 Repeat step 5, continuing to add the top block from each stack onto the right edge of each row through each "round" of blocks.

7 Lay out the webbed set of blocks on the floor or other flat surface. Clip the threads between each row. Press the rows according to your pattern directions. **Note:** You can use this method when there is sashing too!

Finishing

Here are a few guidelines for finishing your quilt, from adding borders to binding.

BORDERS

Follow these steps for perfectly straight borders.

1 Cut the border fabric into strips of the desired width. If your quilt is longer or wider than the length of your strips, piece the strips together and press the seam allowances in one direction.

2 Measure through the center of your quilt, from top to bottom, to determine the correct strip length for the sides of the quilt. Project instructions will usually specify what that length should be, but it's always best to measure your quilt first in case of any discrepancies. (I like to measure by laying my quilt top on the floor and using a stiff measuring tape.) Cut two border strips to the appropriate length.

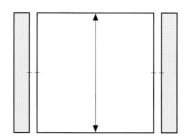

Measure center of quilt, top to bottom. Mark centers.

3 Pin the strips to the sides of your quilt by first matching the centers and ends and then pinning every 3" to 4". When pinning, make sure the border strips and the edges of the quilt are flat and pinned evenly. Stitch in place and press the seam allowances toward the border strips.

4 Measure your quilt top through the center from side to side, including the border strips just added, and cut two strips to that length. Pin the strips

to the top and bottom of your quilt and stitch in place. Press the seam allowances toward the border strips.

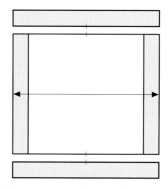

Measure center of quilt, side to side, including border strips. Mark centers.

Cutting Long Strips

It can be challenging to cut border strips that are longer than your ruler or mat, so here's a little trick. First, determine what the border length should be; divide that number in half. Fold the border strips in half lengthwise so that the two layers are slightly longer than the length you just calculated. Place the ruler on the fold and trim.

As an example, let's say you need a 3" × 44½" border strip. Divide 44½" by 2. The result is 22¼", so align the 22¼" mark on your ruler with the folded edge of your fabric and trim.

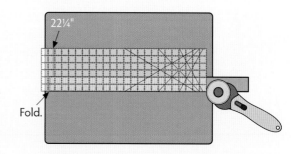

If your strips need to be even longer than twice the length of your ruler (48"), try using the grid marks on your cutting mat. Or measure the first 24" length (48" total for folded fabric), place a pin through the layers of fabric at the end of the ruler, and adjust the ruler from there, adding the additional length needed.

BATTING

With so many different kinds of batting available, choosing the right one can be a challenge. Most commonly, I use 100% bleached cotton batting. It is lightweight and washes up very nicely, with a little shrinkage that gives quilts a wrinkly, antique feel that I love. The batting is available in natural and white; I like to use white to keep my light-colored quilt tops looking extra bright. Talk with staff at your local quilt shop or with your long-arm quilter for more information about the batting that's best for your project.

BACKING

Backing yardage for the projects in this book allow for an extra 3" or 4" on each side of the quilt, depending on the quilt size. For small quilts or table runners, you may be able to get by with less, in order to make best use of your yardage. If you plan to have your quilt professionally machine quilted, check with the quilter to see what dimensions are required. If necessary, sew two or more pieces of backing fabric together.

Making a Scrappy Quilt Back

Scrappy backings are always delightful and a good way to use up your stash. Sew fabric scraps, strips, or blocks together in sections. Keep adding sections, squaring up each one as you go, until you have a quilt back that is approximately 8" bigger than your quilt top. I've made quilt backs before that consisted of just 5" squares, just fat quarters, and different widths of different fabrics to create stripes across the back of my quilt. I've even made a large quilt block to go in the center of my quilt back, as well as a row of blocks across the center. There is no right or wrong way to piece the sections as long as the finished quilt back is bigger than your quilt top. Get creative and have fun. A scrappy back is a great way to give your project a little extra personality!

Black-and-white polka dot fabrics make a fun scrappy backing for Tile Revival (page 55).

BINDING

Unless there's a specific reason to use bias binding (like binding around curves or to make great use of a striped fabric), I like to use double-fold, straight-grain binding. Follow the steps below to add this type of binding.

1 Measure the perimeter of your quilt and add 12" for joining strips and mitering corners. Divide that number by 40 to determine how many strips you need. Cut the necessary number of 2½"-wide strips across the width of the fabric.

Making a Scrappy Binding

If you want a scrappy binding, measure the perimeter of your quilt and add 12" for joining strips and mitering corners. Divide that number by the length of your strips (approximately 20" if using fat quarters, or a shorter length if you're using scraps). That will tell you how many strips you need. Cut the necessary number of strips, 2½" wide by the determined length, from fat quarters or scraps. If you're using strips shorter than 20", or using random lengths, you may need more or fewer strips. Simply piece strips together until you have the needed length (the perimeter of your quilt plus 12"). Follow steps 2–8 to complete the binding.

2 If your binding strips aren't already angled at the ends like mine are in the photo below left, here's how to sew them together and still get an angled seam. (Which is good for distributing the seam allowance bulk when you sew the binding to your quilt.)

Place the end of one strip on top of another with right sides together and at right angles to each other. Offset the strips by ¼" and sew a diagonal line from corner to corner. Trim, leaving a ¼" seam allowance. Repeat until all the strips are joined. Press the seam allowances open to minimize bulk. Then press the long strip in half lengthwise with wrong sides together.

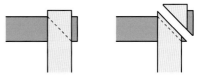

Joining straight-cut strips

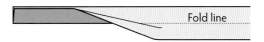

Fold line

3 Align the raw edges of the binding with the raw edges of the quilt on the front. Beginning in the middle of one side of the quilt and leaving about 6" loose, sew the binding to the quilt using a ¼" seam allowance. Use a walking foot on your machine, if you have one, to help feed the layers through evenly. Continue sewing until you are ¼" from the first corner. Stop, adjust your stitch length, and take a couple of stitches in place. Cut the threads.

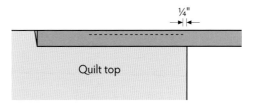

¼"

Quilt top

4 Remove the quilt from under the presser foot. Pivot the quilt and the loose binding in front of you to prepare for sewing the binding to the next side of your quilt. To miter the corners of the binding, fold the binding strip up so that the fold forms a 45° angle and the right edge of the strip is parallel with the next side of the quilt. Then fold the binding down over itself, aligning the raw edges with the quilt edge. Place the corner under the presser foot and insert the needle ¼" from the corner. Stitch in place two times, and then continue sewing. Sew until you are ¼" from the next corner and repeat the process.

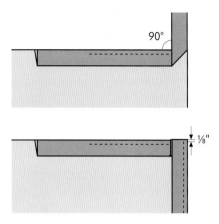

5 When you get back to the side you started on, stop sewing about 10" to 12" from where you began. Stitch in place two times and cut the threads. Remove the quilt from the machine. Overlap the binding ending tail and the starting tail. Then trim the binding ends with a perpendicular cut so that the overlap is the same distance as the width that you cut your binding.

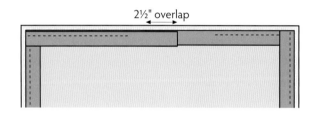

2½" overlap

6 Open up the two ends of the folded binding. Place the tails right sides together at a right angle as shown. Mark a diagonal stitching line from corner to corner and pin the ends together.

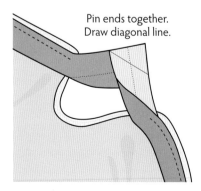

Pin ends together.
Draw diagonal line.

7 Stitch the binding ends together along the marked line. Trim the seam allowances to ¼" and press them open. You can finger-press if you like. Refold the binding, align the edges with the raw edges of the quilt top, and finish sewing the binding onto your quilt.

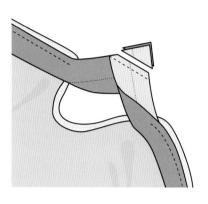

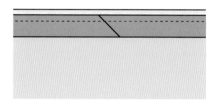

8 Turn the binding to the back of the quilt, being sure to cover your stitching line where you sewed on the binding. Hand stitch the binding to the back of the quilt using a blind stitch. Use a thread color that matches the color of the binding and miter all the corners as you go.

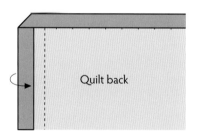

Quilt back

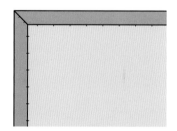

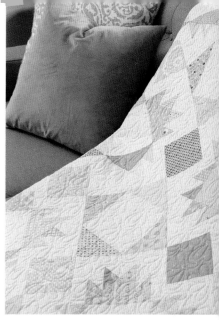

Acknowledgments

Thank you to Riley Blake Designs and Moda Fabrics for contributing fabric yardage for the backs of some of the quilts in this book. I appreciate this and I'm grateful to have been able to work with both of you many times over the years!

Also, a HUGE thank-you to my long-arm quilter, Jen Ostler, for quilting all of the quilts featured in this book. Jen is the most wonderful quilter and sweetest human being! Not only does she do a fantastic, high-quality job, but she is also fast and reasonably priced. The fact that she returns every quilt to me trimmed, tied with ribbon that matches my quilt, and with an individually wrapped chocolate stapled to the receipt is just a million cherries on top! Thank you, thank you, Jen. You are the best!

About the Author

A mber has been quilting for more than 20 years. When she was newly married and living away from her immediate family, with a husband who traveled a lot, she needed a hobby! She asked her grandmother Delma to teach her how to quilt. Delma, an award-winning quilter, was thrilled that someone else in the family wanted to learn how to quilt.

Although it took Amber about three years to finish her first quilt, she was hooked! A decade later, Amber started a quilt-pattern design business called Gigi's Thimble, a tribute to the nickname "Gigi" that Delma's great-grandchildren affectionately used for her. Amber has been blogging and designing quilt patterns since 2009. This is her second quilting book; her first was *Vintage Vibe: Traditional Quilts, Fresh Fabrics* (Martingale, 2014). She has also been published in *Quilts & More* magazine. Amber loves to host quilt-alongs on Instagram, do trunk shows, share tutorials, and teach classes. She often finds inspiration in antique quilts—whether in the design itself or in the maker's fabric selection. She hopes to inspire others to think outside of the box with their own creative color combinations.

Besides Amber's love of quilting, her greatest joys come from being a wife and being a mother to two teenagers. She grew up in Vancouver, Washington, and now resides in Alpine, Utah, where she loves to run and hike. She's a home-design enthusiast and has a bit of wanderlust, hoping to do a lot more traveling as time and money permit.

You can follow Amber's quilting journey on her blog, GigisThimble.com, or on Instagram @gigis_thimble.